WOMEN'S WORLD CUP CLOSE-UP

by Kurt Waldendorf

CAPSTONE PRESS
a capstone imprint

Published by Capstone Press, an imprint of Capstone
1710 Roe Crest Drive, North Mankato, Minnesota 56003
capstonepub.com

Library of Congress Cataloging-in-Publication Data is available on the Library of Congress website

ISBN: 979-8-8752-6965-3 (hardcover)
ISBN: 979-8-8752-6960-8 (paperback)
ISBN: 979-8-8752-6961-5 (ebook PDF)

Summary: Since it was first held in 1991, the Women's World Cup has exploded in popularity. Readers can explore the past, present, and future of this much-loved competition.

Editorial Credits
Editor: Heather DiLorenzo Williams, Designer, Cynthia Della-Rovere, Media Researchers, Courtney Rust, Catherine Guden

Image Credits
Getty: A. Messerschmidt, cover (left), Barrington Coombs, 8–9, Cameron Spencer, 5, Catherine Ivill, 18–19, 24–25, Christian Hofer, cover (right), Henning Bangen/Bongarts, 10–11, John Todd/ISI Photos, 12, Justin Setterfield, cover (middle), 16, 20–21, Maja Hitij, 26–27, Quinn Rooney, 17, 22–23, Robert Cianflone, cover (top), 29, Tim Nwachukwu, 14–15, Topical Press Agency/Hulton Archive, 7

Design Elements
Shutterstock: Arroyan Art, Dmitry Rukhlenko, Donglpix, madorf, Vector-3D

Printed and bound in China. 6459

CONTENTS

Words in **bold** are in the glossary.

CHAPTER 1

A GLOBAL SPOTLIGHT

The Women's World Cup is a truly global event. The tournament brings together the top **national teams** on Earth to compete for the title of world champion. Billions of fans tune in to watch the event on TV and online. Millions more travel to see matches in person.

The event is popular for many reasons. The Women's World Cup spotlights the best players. It brings fans together to cheer for their nation's team. Matches provide **iconic** moments.

The event also inspires girls and women to give soccer a try. In this way, the Women's World Cup does more than crown a champion. It encourages the next generation of competitors.

In 2023, players from Spain celebrated the country's first Women's World Cup win in team history.

CHAPTER 2

MANY YEARS IN THE MAKING

Women have played soccer since the early days of the sport. But many **barriers** had to come down to make the Women's World Cup what it is today.

The Early Years

Modern soccer began in England in the 1800s. The first **international** women's match was in 1881. England and Scotland competed to see which nation had the top team. The sport caught on quickly. During World War I (1914–1918), many men left to become soldiers. In England, their factory jobs were filled by the women left behind. And like the men before them, these women joined **club teams** in their spare time. Matches drew huge crowds.

After the war, things changed. Men returned to their jobs and their club teams. League organizers worried women's soccer would hurt ticket sales for the men's game. Some people didn't think women should play soccer at all. A ban went into effect in England. The ban kept women from playing soccer. Other countries also put bans in place. Women in Norway, Brazil, and Germany weren't allowed to compete, either.

Women compete in a charity soccer game in England in 1914.

In the first 50 years after Title IX passed, the number of girls participating in school sports went from 300,000 to more than 3 million.

Sudden Shifts

Bans on women's soccer lasted many years. Still, women found ways to form teams. In 1970, Italy hosted the first big international women's tournament. Teams from seven countries took part. The event was a hit. A crowd of 40,000 watched Denmark take on Italy in the final. A year later, the event was even bigger. The tournament was held in Mexico. More than 100,000 people filled the stands to watch the final between Denmark and Mexico.

After the tournaments, things started to change. England ended its ban. The United States passed a new law. It was called Title IX. Title IX helped make men's and women's sports more equal. U.S. schools offered **scholarships** to women to play sports. The law helped the United States produce top women's soccer players. It also made women's soccer more competitive around the world.

Becoming Official

More barriers for women's soccer came down in the 1990s. The group that organized the Men's World Cup created a women's event for the first time. The Fédération Internationale de Football Association (FIFA) scheduled the first women's tournament for 1991. It took place 61 years after the first men's World Cup.

Women's Soccer in the Olympics

The Olympic Games added women's soccer in 1996. The change was big for the sport. Matches drew record in-person crowds. The Olympics reached a wider television audience too. People who weren't soccer fans tuned in to see their nation go for gold. After the event, more countries developed women's soccer programs to compete at future events.

Still, FIFA was worried people might not be interested in the event. FIFA did not call the tournament a "World Cup." But the tournament was a success. More than 500,000 people attended matches. FIFA held another event four years later. The tournament officially became the Women's World Cup.

Although they placed fourth during the first Women's World Cup in 1991, Germany has remained one of the best teams in women's soccer.

Brandi Chastain celebrates her penalty kick, which gave the U.S. Women's National Team (USWNT) the win in the 1999 Women's World Cup final.

Another Level

The first two Women's World Cups made the tournament official. The third tournament, held in 1999, made it a fan favorite. It was the biggest event yet. The tournament took place in the United States. Fans filled huge stadiums across the country. TV stations broadcast matches around the world.

The teams delivered an exciting tournament. The final match was between China and the United States. After playing to a 0–0 tie, the match went to **penalty kicks**. Brandi Chastain knocked in the winning goal for the United States. About 90,000 people cheered from the stands. The win grabbed the attention of people in the United States and beyond. It showed how exciting the Women's World Cup could be.

Several current and past members of the USWNT celebrate the agreement signed in 2022 that stated women's players would receive pay equal to men's players.

Growing the Game

The 1999 Women's World Cup changed the game. Millions of girls and women were inspired to join the sport. As a result, more and more countries built strong teams. Germany won its first Women's World Cup in 2003. They won it again in 2007. Japan claimed its first title in 2011.

The first pro women's soccer leagues started in the United States. Women on the USWNT became celebrities. They brought attention to important issues. In 2022, the team won the right to be paid as much as the men's athletes.

FAST FACT

The National Women's Soccer League (NWSL) in the United States is among the top pro leagues in the world. But it isn't just for American athletes. Players from around the globe sign with NWSL clubs. About 40 different national teams have players in the league.

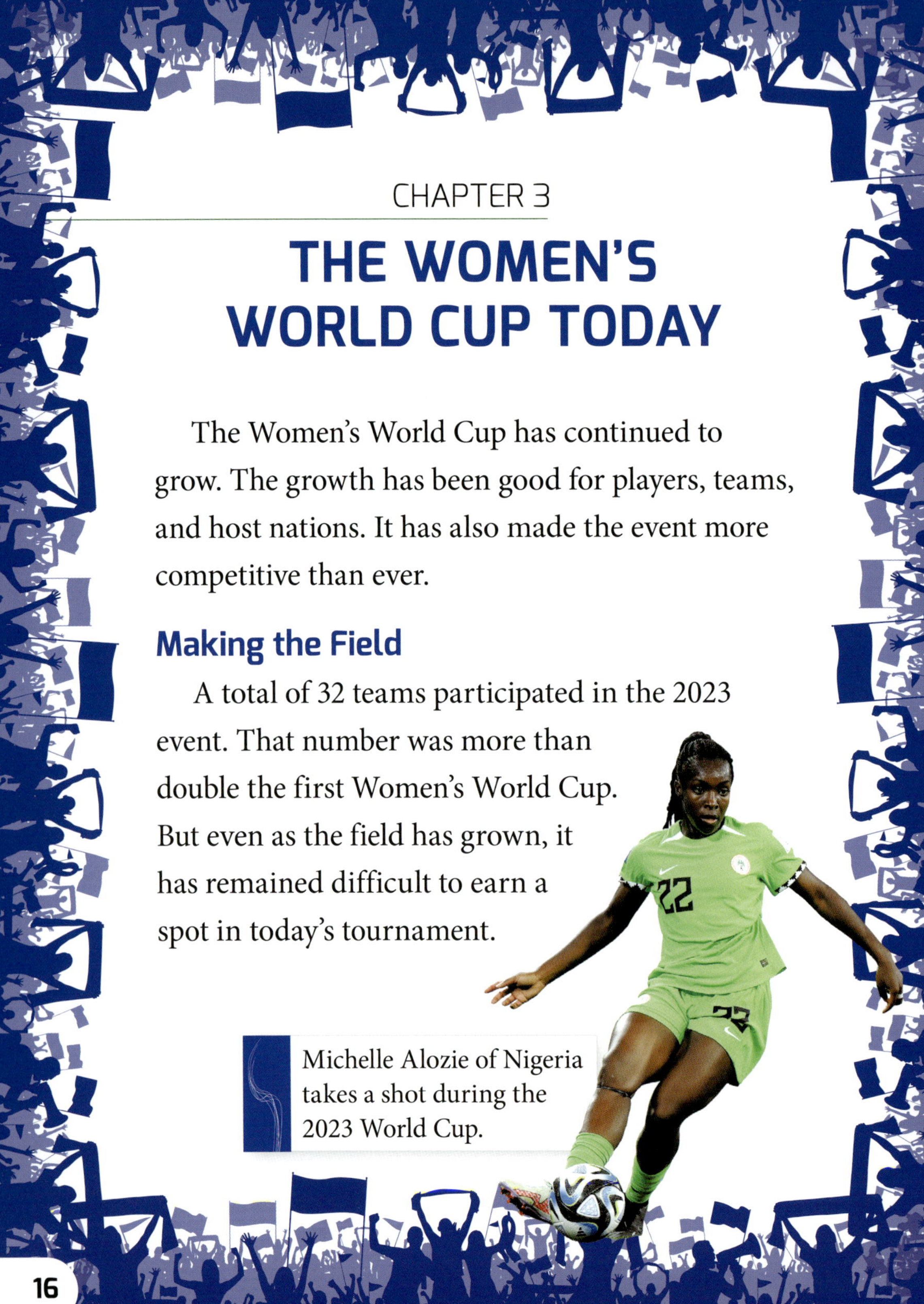

CHAPTER 3

THE WOMEN'S WORLD CUP TODAY

The Women's World Cup has continued to grow. The growth has been good for players, teams, and host nations. It has also made the event more competitive than ever.

Making the Field

A total of 32 teams participated in the 2023 event. That number was more than double the first Women's World Cup. But even as the field has grown, it has remained difficult to earn a spot in today's tournament.

Michelle Alozie of Nigeria takes a shot during the 2023 World Cup.

About 200 countries have women's national teams. FIFA divides the teams into six regions. In the years leading up to the tournament, each region holds **qualifying** matches. Only the top teams earn a spot. As of the 2023 tournament, just seven nations had qualified for every Women's World Cup: Brazil, Germany, Japan, Nigeria, Norway, Sweden, and the United States.

Alyssa Naeher of the UNWNT makes a spectacular save in a 2023 Women's World Cup match against Sweden.

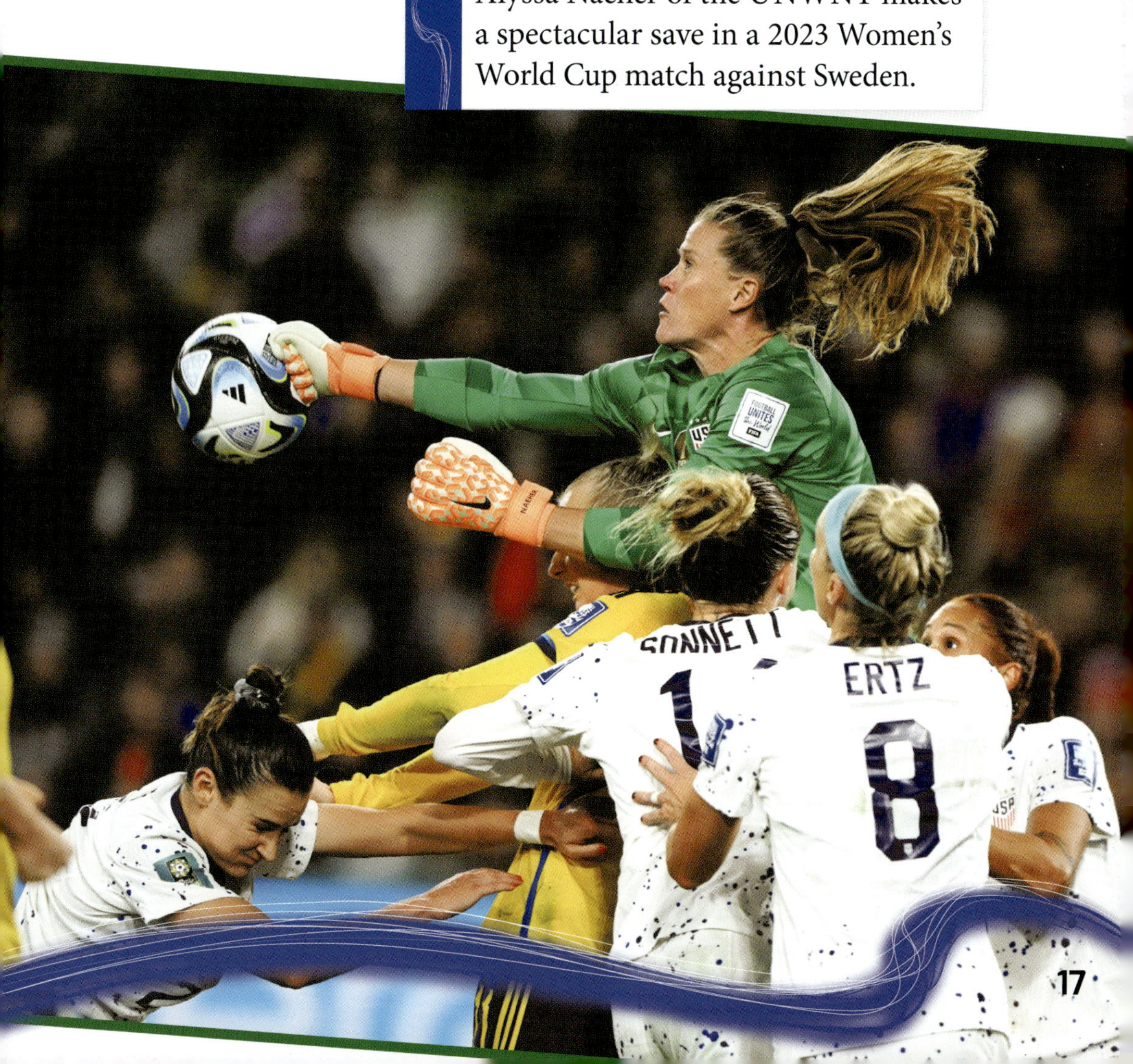

Choosing a Host

Countries also compete to host the tournament. They create plans for the event called bids. FIFA picks the plan they like best. After the host is selected, the work begins. Countries make improvements to stadiums. They build hotels for visitors to stay in and roads so people can get around. New Zealand and Australia both hosted the 2023 event. Preparing for the tournament created 38,000 jobs in those countries. The event brought in around 2 million visitors.

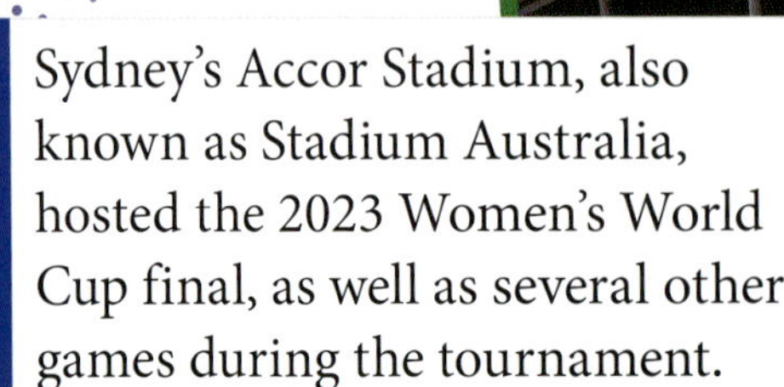

Sydney's Accor Stadium, also known as Stadium Australia, hosted the 2023 Women's World Cup final, as well as several other games during the tournament.

Hosting doesn't just help the country. It also helps the sport. After the 2023 event, participation from girls and women spiked in both host countries. Money was set aside to grow leagues for all ages and skill levels.

Player Preparation

Players train their whole lives to play in the Women's World Cup. They work on skills such as dribbling, passing, and shooting. They learn game strategies so they can make the right move at the right time. Players show their hard work while competing for club teams. National teams pick the top players from club teams to represent their country.

About 10 days before the tournament, the final **rosters** are set. A total of 736 players travel to the tournament. In the days leading up to the matches, teams study their opponents. They come up with a game plan. Then they take the field.

FAST FACT

Players reach the Women's World Cup at many ages. The youngest player to compete was Casey Phair. She was 16 when she played for South Korea in 2023. The oldest player to compete was Miraildes Maciel Mota of Brazil. She competed in the 2019 tournament at age 41.

South Korea's Casey Phair (left) challenges Germany's Marina Hegering (right) during the 2023 World Cup.

Narrowing the Field

With the participants set, 32 nations start to face off. During the **group stage**, each team competes against the other three teams in their group. The stage ensures every team plays at least three matches. The top two teams from each group move on to the knockout rounds.

In the knockout rounds, a single loss ends a team's hopes of winning the title. Teams cannot tie in these rounds. If the score is tied at the end of extra time, the match goes to penalty kicks. In penalty kicks, a single strike can win the match.

Australia's women's team came in fourth at the 2023 World Cup, their best finish of all time.

Staying Ready

The Women's World Cup lasts for one month. The winning team plays seven matches. That doesn't leave much time between games. Players need to recover. Teams need to plan for their next opponent. Teams also have to travel to their next match. In 2023, Ireland's team traveled 5,100 miles (8,208 km) between group stage matches.

Crowning a Champion

The two unbeaten teams in the knockout rounds face off in the final. The winner becomes world champion. Only a few nations have earned the title. Following the 2023 event, the United States had the most Women's World Cup wins with four. Germany had two. Spain, Norway, and Japan each had one.

Individuals also get awards. The Golden Ball goes to the most valuable player. In 2023, the prize went to Aitana Bonmatí of Spain. The Golden Boot goes to the player who scores the most goals. The top goaltender gets the Golden Glove. In 2023, Japan's Hinata Miyazawa took home the Golden Boot. England's Mary Earps won the Golden Glove.

FAST FACT

Kristine Lilly has the record for most Women's World Cup matches. She took the field 30 times for the United States. Brazil's Marta is the top Women's World Cup scorer all-time. She found the back of the net 17 times.

Aitana Bonmatí (left) and Mary Earps (right) show off their individual awards after the final game of the 2023 World Cup.

Kelley O’Hara, Alex Morgan, and Allie Long (left to right) kiss the World Cup trophy after their 2019 win. The three players have worked alongside their teammates to bring equality to women’s soccer.

Sharing the Success

Many barriers have come down since the first Women's World Cup. During the 1991 event, there was no prize money. U.S players were given only $15 per day to spend at the tournament. Over time, players helped bring about changes. In 2007, prize money was introduced. And for the 2023 tournament, every player made at least $30,000.

Still, players are still pushing for more equality and better treatment. Much of the tournament's prize money goes to soccer organizers. Players are pressing for more of the prize money to go to tournament participants instead of to each country's soccer organization. They are also calling for better conditions at the tournament and longer breaks after the event. By backing change, they want to make the Women's World Cup better for future generations.

CHAPTER 4

AN INCLUSIVE FUTURE

The future of the Women's World Cup looks bright. More and more girls are trying the sport. More countries are putting money into women's teams. The results are showing on the field. The 2023 tournament wasn't just the biggest yet. It was also the most diverse. Eight nations made their first-ever appearance in the Women's World Cup. Teams such as South Africa and Jamaica earned their first wins. Spain won its first title.

Different countries are also hosting the event. Brazil was selected as the host for the 2027 Women's World Cup. It was the first South American country chosen to host. With new participants and hosts, the Women's World Cup has positioned itself to inspire a new generation of young athletes around the world.

Jamaica advanced to the Round of 16 in only their second-ever Women's World Cup appearance in 2023.

GLOSSARY

barriers (BAR-ee-uhrz)—obstacles that stop movement or access

club teams (KLUHB TEEMZ)—sports squads that represent organizations

group stage (GROOP STAYJ)—part of a tournament in which teams play multiple matches against a small set of competitors

iconic (eye-KAH-nik)—widely viewed as perfectly capturing the meaning or spirit of something or someone

international (in-tur-NASH-uh-nuhl)—including more than one nation

national teams (NASH-uh-nuhl TEEMZ)—sports squads that represent their countries

penalty kicks (PEN-uhl-tee KICKZ)—free kicks awarded to the offense when the defense commits a penalty

qualifying (KWAHL-uh-fye-ing)—determining which teams will play in the World Cup

rosters (ROSS-turs)—lists of players on teams

scholarships (SKOL-ur-ships)—awards of money that are given to students to pay for school

READ MORE

Berglund, Bruce R. *Soccer GOATs: The Greatest Athletes of All Time*. Minneapolis: Capstone, 2024.

Hanlon, Luke. *Alex Morgan*. Minneapolis: ABDO, 2024.

McDougall, Chrös. *The Best Women's Players of World Soccer*. Minneapolis: ABDO, 2024.

INTERNET SITES

ESPN: FIFA Women's World Cup
www.espn.com/soccer/league/_/name/fifa.wwc

FIFA Women's World Cup 2027
www.fifa.com/en/tournaments/womens/womensworldcup/brazil-2027

Sports Illustrated Kids: Soccer
www.sikids.com/tag/soccer

INDEX

About the Author

Kurt Waldendorf is the author of more than a dozen books for children. When he's not writing or editing, he enjoys indoor rock climbing and running along the shore of Lake Michigan with his dog. He lives in Chicago.